After Adultery

Published in cooperation with the

CHRISTIAN COUNSELING &
EDUCATIONAL FOUNDATION

Susan Lutz, Editor

Other booklets, as well as video tapes, DVDs,
CDs and audio cassettes, may be ordered
through www.ccef.org.

Christian Counseling &
Educational Foundation

RESTORING CHRIST *to* COUNSELING &
COUNSELING *to the* CHURCH

After Adultery

Robert D. Jones

New
Growth
Press

Unless otherwise indicated, all Scripture quotations are from the HOLY BIBLE, NEW INTERNATIONAL VERSION®. Copyright © 1973, 1978, 1984 by International Bible Society. Used by permission of Zondervan Publishing House. All rights reserved.

Printed in Canada.

Library of Congress Cataloging-in-Publication Data

10-Digit ISBN 0-9770807-9-X
13-Digit ISBN 978-0-9770807-9-3

You probably picked up this booklet because adultery has jolted your marriage or the marriage of a family member or friend. You knew these things happened; you just never expected them to happen to you.

Let me assure you that you are not alone. Infidelity is more common than you might imagine. Be it an illicit kiss or full sexual union, even Christians have violated their vows to forsake all others and cling only to their spouse.

Maybe you're the offended partner.[1] You've felt many of the common responses.

- Anger: "I hate my spouse for what he did." "I despise the woman he slept with."
- Despair, hopelessness: "I'll never get over this. My life is over."
- Fear: "What's going to happen next? What do I do now?"
- Jealousy: "I can't believe he picked her over me."
- Regret, guilt: "I know I've failed; I drove him into her arms."
- Relief: "I suspected it; I'm glad it's out. We've been living a lie too long."
- Revenge: "I'll get him for this. I'll hire the best attorney. . . ."
- Embarrassment, shame: "How can I face my family? What will my church say?"

Or maybe you're the offender, and you're having your own struggles (with little permission to feel them):

- Guilt: "I have sinned; I really blew it this time."
- Anger: "If she had been a better wife, this wouldn't have happened." "I can't believe my buddy told my wife."
- Fear: "What will my wife do to me? Will she forgive me, or is this the end? What will my church and family do?"
- Despair, suicide: "I see no way out. My life is over. I may as well end it."
- Relief: "Deep down I'm glad I got caught. I've been living a lie. Now it's over."
- Embarrassment, shame: "How will I face anyone ever again? I need to move away."

Did you notice the overlap in the two lists? Crises like adultery reveal the core struggles in every human heart. At the end of the day, every one of us – offender, offended, or caring helper – needs the same Redeemer to minister to our particular battles.

THE STARTING POINT: THE GOD OF HOPE

Where do we begin to deal biblically with this marital crisis?

Ask God to help you believe his promises.

No matter how well you know your Bible, in the coming days you will need fresh servings of daily bread. Don't rest on past grace. Believe that God wants to meet you now in new ways.

We don't know whether the writer of Psalm 46 envisioned an actual earthquake, an enemy invasion, or some other tragedy. But his imagery captures the devastation many spouses feel when they discover their partner's unfaithfulness:

> God is our refuge and strength, an ever-present help in trouble. Therefore we will not fear, though the earth give way and the mountains fall into the heart of the sea, though its waters roar and foam and the mountains quake with their surging. (vv.1-3)

This was Lisa's experience.[2] "I fell apart when I found out what Tim had done. The bottom of my life suddenly dropped out, and I was free-falling into the darkness." Max put it more starkly: "Sara was my life. And now my life is over."

What is our hope? God has spoken: "God is our refuge and strength, an ever-present help in trouble" (v.1). God's presence and power are yours in the midst of adultery's wreckage. He is right there, smack in the middle of your life, to help you (v.5). Twice, the psalm bursts forth with hope and assurance: "The LORD Almighty is with us; the God of Jacob is our fortress" (vv.7, 11). He is present. He is powerful. He cares.

In Genesis 50 Joseph, a victim of multiple betrayals, grasped God's hope as he declared to his offenders, "You intended to harm me, but God intended it for good . . ." (50:20). The apostle Paul assures suffering Christians that "in all things God works for the good of those who love him," a good he defines as making us like Jesus Christ (Rom. 8:28-29). Whatever the action or intention of an unfaithful spouse, God has a life-changing agenda for you, a positive, redemptive purpose in this situation.

What if you are the adulterer? Is there hope for you? Hosea's marriage in Hosea 1-3 is an adulterous union that was restored by grace. As the observant reader learns, Hosea's unfaithful partner is a picture of our own spiritual infidelity against our husband, Jesus Christ. The Bible abounds with promises of God's forgiveness.[3]

More than this, the God who forgives can also restore. Listen to his promise to those he exiled to a foreign land because of their sin: "For I know the plans I have for you," declares the LORD, "plans to prosper you and not to harm you, plans to give you hope and a future" (Jer. 29:11; see also Joel 2:12-13, 25). God offers prosperity, safety, hope, and a future to a once-unfaithful people.

In other words, you have a *Redeemer*. God promises you hope and help in Jesus to rebuild your life. He loves *you* and has a glorious plan for *your* life, even if your spouse never forsakes his infidelity or never forgives you for yours.

Commit yourself to pleasing God by believing and following Jesus, regardless of your spouse's commitments.

The challenge is simple yet piercing: Whether you are the offender or the offended, do you want to follow Jesus more than anything, even more than restoring your marriage? Is God your highest aim?

I don't pretend that faith and obedience are easy for you right now, especially if your spouse is not seeking to please God. If your spouse doesn't seem to follow Jesus, or does not do so with proper pace or passion, you will be tempted to give up your own pursuit of Jesus. "If he is not going to work on it, or even go with me to a counselor, what's the use of even trying? Why should I be the only one to try?"

Or worse, you may become proud and self-righteous. "I may not be perfect, but at least I'm willing to work on it, which is more than I can say about my spouse." Even the offender is in danger here: "Yeah, I messed up, but at least I am the one [read, the superior one] willing to work on things."

God's answer, whether you are the offender or the offended, is that you should believe and follow Jesus right now because he is worthy, without subtly bargaining with God. The Christian recognizes that "Christ's love compels us . . ., that those who live should no longer live for themselves but for him who died for them and was raised again" (2 Cor. 5:14-15). You can't make your faith and obedience conditional on your partner's response.

Here's how I explain it in an opening counseling session:

> If you [looking at the offended wife] seek to believe and follow Jesus according to the biblical counsel I give you, I can guarantee that you will become a more godly woman, wife, and (if she has children) mom. But I can guarantee you *nothing* about your marriage.
>
> If you [turning to the offending husband] seek to believe and follow Jesus according to the biblical counsel I give you, I can guarantee that you will become a more godly man, husband, and (if he has children) dad. But I can guarantee you *nothing* about your marriage.
>
> But if *both* of you [turning to both partners] seek to follow Christ, I can guarantee

something about your marriage, that you two together will have a godly, growing, fulfilling marriage.

Do you believe that? Jesus not only can restore your marriage but make it stronger than it was before. We don't want to merely revert to the pre-infidelity state of your marriage. In Christ, God provides something better.

Here's why: Our God delights in making broken things better than they were. Like a severed steel joint strengthened by the welding process, the Redeemer can weld your severed marriage into something sturdy. The lives of many "welded" couples attest to this. The God of new birth, new life, and new beginnings offers something more than restoration; he offers transformation.

Recognize common enemies of the welding process.

- Competing counsel from friends and family. Assume their motives are good; don't assume their advice is biblical.
- Gossip. Be careful with whom you discuss the infidelity. Go first to your pastor or biblical counselor to get counsel on who needs to know and what you should say.
- Rash decisions. Seek biblical counsel right away – before you move out, visit an attorney, or confront your spouse's "lover." A hasty decision may complicate the problem and bring later regrets.
- Despair, cynicism. It's easy to give up and conclude, "Rebuilding the marriage

may be an option for others but not for us." Beware of the unbelief and sinister arrogance that views your situation as somehow beyond God's grace.

THE PATH OF BELIEVING AND FOLLOWING JESUS

What will rebuilding your life and marriage look like? The following can serve you, your spouse, and your pastor or counselor as a roadmap for the welding process.[4] Each partner must pursue his own path, seeking to please God while depending on his strength.

Offender

1. Break the adulterous relationship immediately.
2. Admit the facts; disclose honestly.
3. Confess to God, spouse, and appropriate others the adultery and the deception/lies, and seek their forgiveness.
4. Develop and implement a specific action plan for godly change.
5. Believe the gospel and move forward, continuing this action plan.

Offended

1. Find your security and identity in Jesus Christ, not in your spouse or marriage.
2. View this trial biblically; see God's sovereign, wise, loving purposes.
3. Forgive your spouse attitudinally and unconditionally in light of the gospel.
4. Forgive your spouse relationally and transactionally if he repents.
5. Realize the process nature of these matters; deal with bad memories when they arise.

If you have committed adultery, what is God calling you to do?

1. Break the adulterous relationship immediately.

You must begin with an unconditional, immediate break with your adulterous partner. No protracted, step-by-step disengagement is acceptable. Your marriage and your eternal soul are too important to permit any delay or bargaining. Whatever the cost or the anticipated impact on the other person,[5] you must make a swift, forceful break.

Let your pastor or a mature Christian friend help you by holding you accountable (or even getting on the phone with you) when you call the other party to announce your breakup.

Do you feel the urgency of this indispensable step? If your right eye leads you to sin, gouge it out and throw it away; if your right hand offends you, cut it off and throw it away (Matt. 5:29-30). Avoid the temptress's pathway (Prov. 5). Run from Potiphar's wife (Gen. 39). Flee youthful lusts (2 Tim. 2:22).

2. Admit the facts; disclose honestly.

I recommend a two-stage confession: An initial, honest disclosure of the facts (here), followed by a reflective, thorough, God-centered confession (Step 3). This approach recognizes the importance of an immediate acknowledgment to your spouse and pastor or counselor. It also recognizes that a more thorough and careful repentance is still needed.

What does this initial disclosure look like? You need to tell your spouse and your pastor (or church leader) what you have done. In some cases your spouse already knows; in many cases she suspects. Your honest admission will be the first step in rebuilding trust. Obviously, your repentance will be more believable if you volunteer the information – the whole story – rather than wait to be caught.

If you are afraid to tell your spouse (an understandable fear), start with your pastor, a mature friend (same gender), or trusted church leader. He can help you approach your spouse. He may even go with you to support you and help your spouse handle the news.

How much should you share? As a general rule, you should tell everything your spouse asks or might need to know to move toward forgiving and trusting you. As the offender, you may need to err on the side of over-disclosure. You will also need to allow her unhindered freedom to check your phone bills, cell phone memory, email folders, and so on. (If your spouse seems absorbed in detailed questions or seems unreasonably ruled by unwise curiosity, you can appeal to her or to your counselor for help.)

Come clean completely. She may or may not forgive you. But if she later discovers you have held back or minimized important facts, the odds of her forgiving and trusting you severely diminish. If the adultery itself does not end the marriage, your half-truths may kill it.

3. Confess to God, spouse, and appropriate others the adultery and the deception/lies, and seek their forgiveness.

This step comes days or even weeks later, after you have broken off the relationship. You have gone through counseling with your pastor or counselor, prayerfully meditating on and applying Scripture, and reflecting on your dual sins of immorality and lying, along with other ways you have sinned against your spouse.

Having severed the adulterous relationship and admitted your sin, the task now is to see your sin the way God sees it and to deal with it his way, through repentance and confession. See with shame what your sin did to Jesus on the cross; see by faith what he did to your sin on that same cross.

Be ruthlessly honest! Ask God to search your heart and expose your sin in its depth and breadth (Ps. 139:23-24; Heb. 4:12-13). Let God's Word show you the ugly spots that you ignore. Don't be like the man who told me, "I may not have done a great job in confessing, but at least I'm addressing the things my wife is most upset about."

To whom must confession be made? Start with God. All sin, including sexual sin, is first and foremost against God. David recognized this after his adultery: "Against you, you only, have I sinned and done what is evil in your sight, so that you are proved right when you speak and justified when you judge" (Ps. 51:4; see also Gen. 39:9; 1 Thess. 4:5-7).

Go to God in prayer, seeing the depth of your sin. Ask him to forgive you for Jesus' sake. Study passages that portray true repentance: Daniel 9, Ezra 9, and Nehemiah 9, in which godly men voice Israel's confession; along with Psalms 32 and 51, the two psalms tied to David's adultery.

You must then confess your sins to your spouse and seek her forgiveness.[6] In some cases you may need to confess to others.[7]

10

What must be confessed? Obviously, you must confess the sexual sin itself and any relational activities and conversational intimacies that led up to it. But what is equally important (and for many spouses is more important) is confessing the surrounding deception and lies. Your lying likely hurt her more than the sexual act. It is a more formidable obstacle to forgiveness and marital trust.

"I could have handled the news of his adultery," Ginger told her pastor. "But for him to lie to me – to look me in the face and deny there was anything going on, to sleep with me on Tuesday after he slept with her on Monday – that's too much for me to bear. I can forgive an adulterer but not a liar."

4. Develop and implement a specific action plan for godly change.

Confession is not enough. Change must occur. As the wisdom writer said, "He who conceals his sins does not prosper, but whoever confesses and renounces them finds mercy" (Prov. 28:13).

What should be included in this action plan? Based on your comprehensive self-examination, you need to determine how you will change, how you will handle temptation, whom you will invite into your life for accountability, what disciplines you will incorporate, how you will relate to your wife, and so on. Your pastor or counselor can help you draft the plan, but it must come from you. It must be the visible fruit of your inward repentance.

Your plan must be doable and realistic. "I'll never talk to a woman on the job" or "I'll read my Bible for one hour every morning" is not possible or even wise. It must be specific, with concrete, measurable action steps. It must have an accountability component, with the names of your pastor and other godly men who will help you (and whom your wife may contact to share her concerns).

5. Believe the gospel and move forward, continuing the action plan.

You have no guarantee that your spouse will forgive you. But you do have the guarantee – sworn to you on oath, sealed with Christ's blood – that Almighty God will forgive you.

This means that you must not let any lingering guilt cripple you further.[8] The temptation will be strong if your spouse won't forgive you. While you need to be patient and recognize the challenges your sins have brought her, you must not confuse your spouse's forgiveness with God's. God does not have the struggles of progressive sanctification that she does; he doesn't grow in his ability to forgive or "need more time." His forgiveness was finally and forever sealed in the death of his Son, and it comes to us as a perfect and immediate announcement in the gospel.

THE OFFENDED PARTNER'S PATH

What will it look like for you, the offended party, to believe and follow Jesus?

1. Find your security and identity in Jesus Christ, not in your spouse or marriage.

For most people, their spouse's unfaithfulness can shatter their world and unhinge their life. But the true foundation for a Christian's life is not his spouse or marriage or the blessings they bring. Our life is built on Christ.

Infidelity, however, challenges that claim. It screams out that your life is over, that all that is

12

precious is now gone, that there is no hope.

What must you do? Believe the gospel. Rise up and declare that your life is not built on anything or anyone other than your Lord Jesus. Listen to these powerful reminders:

- "Though my father and mother [or spouse!] forsake me, the LORD will receive me" (Ps. 27:10).
- "Whom have I in heaven but you? And earth has nothing I desire besides you. My flesh and my heart may fail, but God is the strength of my heart and my portion forever" (Ps. 73:25-26).
- ". . . You will leave me all alone. Yet I am not alone, for my Father is with me" (John 16:32, Jesus speaking to his disciples on the eve of his crucifixion).

Sondra was abandoned by a man who chose another woman and a daily six-pack over Sondra and God. Sitting with my wife and me on our patio, she shared a remarkable insight: "I didn't see it then. But I see it now. I had made Don the center of my life. God in his sovereign love allowed my foundation to be torn away so that I might learn to make the Lord the center of my life."

2. View this trial biblically. See God's sovereign, wise, loving purpose.

While the type or extent of the adultery may vary – the one night stand v. the entangled, emotional relationship v. the sexual addict or predator – the bottom line is the same: You have been sinned against. You are suffering.

Viewed this way, your whole Bible suddenly opens before you. Passage upon passage – whole books like the Psalms, 1 Peter, James, or Revelation – speak to believers who are sinned against. Hymn after hymn reminds sufferers that the Lord's Word is our firm foundation and that, because of Christ, it is well with our souls, though Satan should buffet or trials should come.

Consider, for example, a famous text like Romans 8:28-29, which tells us that God's sovereign, wise, and loving purpose in all things is to make us more like Jesus. How might God use a trial like adultery to increase your Christ-likeness?

- It can draw you closer to the Lord. I've known offended spouses whose Bible reading and prayer became more fervent during the crisis.
- It gives you opportunity to experience, in part, the suffering, loneliness, and betrayal our Lord Jesus experienced as our Savior and High Priest.
- Our Redeemer uses trials like this to expose our remaining sin, to uncover blind spots and pockets of remnant ungodliness. This does not mean that you caused your spouse to sin; the truth is that God lovingly uses the fires of affliction to burn away the dross in our lives.
- God's comfort to you in your trial will equip you to be a wiser, more sensitive friend to those with similar marital hardships (2 Cor. 1:3-4).

How do you weather this storm? The apostle Peter's counsel to those who are sinned against can guide you. "So then, those who suffer according to God's will should commit themselves to their faithful Creator and continue to do good" (1 Peter 4:19; see also 2:21-23). Trust God (which includes entrusting your life, your spouse, and your marriage into God's hands) and do what's right.

3. Forgive your spouse attitudinally and unconditionally in light of the gospel.

When we examine the Bible's teaching on forgiveness,[9] it's helpful to distinguish two levels. We cultivate attitudinal or heart forgiveness before God concerning all offenders; we extend transacted or granted forgiveness to those offenders who repent. The first level is unconditional and involves a heart commitment before God in his presence (Mark 11:25; Luke 23:34a). The second level is connected to the offender's repentance and involves a promise to him, in his presence, not to hold his sins against him (Luke 17:3b-4; Acts 2:36-41).[10]

What does attitudinal forgiveness look like? It means that you release your adulterous spouse from your judgment and entrust him to God (1 Peter 2:22-23; 4:19; Rom. 12:19). It means that you empty your heart of bitterness (Eph. 4:31-32). And it means that you become willing to grant transacted forgiveness (Step 4 below) and reconcile the relationship if the offender repents (Matt. 18:12-14, 15-17; Luke 17:3-4).

How can this happen? Only by meditating on the gospel. As the One who forgave your multi-million dollar sin debt against him (Matt. 18:21-35), God is your motive and your model for forgiving others. You forgive your spouse because God forgave you,

15

and in the same way God forgave you. "Be kind and compassionate to one another, forgiving each other, just as in Christ God forgave you" (Eph. 4:32).

4. Forgive your spouse relationally and transactionally, if he repents.

As your heart grasps gospel forgiveness, you will become open to relational reconciliation with your unfaithful spouse. As he confesses his sins and seeks your forgiveness, this means that you proceed to forgive him and to reconcile your relationship, just as God in Christ has forgiven you and reconciled his relationship with you. Apart from exceptional cases, this means reconciling your marriage with your repentant partner.[11]

Here, it is most helpful to view the essence of forgiveness as a promise. God's forgiveness involves his decision, declaration, and promise, on account of Jesus Christ, to not hold our sins against us. Like God, you decide, declare, and promise, because of Christ, not to raise the matter again. Ken Sande captures this dynamic with four promises:[12]

- I will not dwell on your sin.
- I will not bring up your sin and use it against you.
- I will not talk to others about your sin.
- I will not allow your sin to stand between us or hinder our personal relationship.

While the decision to forgive should come in response to the offender's confession, I realize this may be a difficult decision. Keep meditating on the gospel. In the coming days, amid temptations to

16

forget or renege on your promises, you will need to frequently recall and renew them and to repent of your violations. The need for grace is obvious.

5. Realize the process nature of these matters; deal with bad memories when they arise.

Living a life of forgiveness, learning to trust your spouse in a proper way, and dealing with recurring memories of his sin can be a hard task.

Don't panic. Don't be surprised if memories resurface. They will. Despite your commitment not to dwell on your partner's sins, thoughts may intrude without welcome or warning. Dozens of cues may trigger this, not the least of which will be marital sexual activity. While there are some situational triggers you may be able to avoid (e.g., you can drive a different route), many are unavoidable (e.g., you cannot eliminate the other woman's name from the English language or stop a couple in your church from giving it to their newborn daughter).

What should you do when memories arise?

- Pray. Ask God to guard your mind from these remembrances of a past sin.
- Rehearse the gospel promises. Remember Christ's work on the cross to pay for and remove all your sins.
- Renew before God your promises of forgiveness. If you displayed a lack of forgiveness toward the spouse you forgave, you must repent, seek his forgiveness, and re-affirm yours.

- Focus on key biblical truths about God and his Son Jesus and turn your energies toward prayer and service toward others, including your spouse.

God has destined every one of his sons and daughters to final glory, but he has not designed a painless pathway or instantaneous glorification. Progressive growth – including wrestling with troubling memories – is God's way of holiness for you and your spouse.

NEXT STEPS: COMING TOGETHER

As you and your spouse walk these paths, recognizing God's forgiving grace and depending on his enabling grace, your marriage is in the process of rebuilding.

The next step – if and when you both are ready – is to recommit yourselves to the marriage covenant and to explore the marital problems that existed prior to the infidelity. The affair did not arise in a vacuum; good marriages seldom beget adultery. You and your spouse will need to deal with the individual "fruit and root" problems that precipitated and accompanied the adultery. Christ-centered, biblical counseling should then follow.

Another question you will need to address – in both the crisis and the rebuilding phases – is this: What should you and your spouse say to other people?

There are, of course, many variables: How much the other person already knows, the degree you view him as trustworthy and confidential, his level of spiritual maturity, how much contact you will likely have with him, etc.

The bigger issue is to agree together on what you say about what has happened. Discuss and agree what you will report and to whom. Talk together about how you will respond to the friend, relative, or church member who asks about what happened.

CONCLUSION

These last steps in the offender's and the offended's paths call you to persevere in believing and following Jesus, in light of his grace. If you were the unfaithful one, believe the gospel promises and live out your action plan of change. If you were sinned against, renew your promises to forgive your spouse and deal properly with recurring bad memories.

Let's close with the hope-filled words of one reunited-by-grace couple:

> If you had told me one year earlier – when my husband's affair was uncovered – that we would be together today, I would have laughed at you. If you had told me our marriage would be strong, I would have called you cruel. But that's exactly what God has brought out. All is not ideal; he is far from a perfect husband, and doubts and memories still invade me. But what we have learned about ourselves and about our Lord is priceless. Praise God, who really does redeem dirty things and makes them shine.

NOTES

[1] There are various ways to describe the respective marital partners, e.g., betrayer v. victim, or guilty v. innocent. My offender v. offended language seeks to be less emotionally charged, to avoid wrong connotations about victimhood or innocence, and to focus on repenting of and forgiving the offense. For the sake of writing simplicity and consistency, I am using male pronouns for the offender and female pronouns for the offended. But, of course, either spouse may have committed the adultery.

[2] Counselee names are pseudonyms. Some represent actual cases; some are composites.

[3] Read Psalms 32; 51; 103; and 130; Micah 7:18-20; Colossians 1:13-14; and 2:13-14.

[4] I do not think all marriage problems require a third party or skilled counselor, but cases of infidelity generally do. If you are part of a Christ-centered, Bible-believing church, contact your church leaders, who can counsel you or connect you with a biblical counselor.

[5] Let your pastor or biblical counselor help you deal with problems that sometimes emerge but that go beyond the scope of this booklet: What if the other partner in adultery threatens suicide, or becomes pregnant, or is a coworker, supervisor, or employee, or a relative or in-law?

[6] I highly recommend Ken Sande, *The Peacemaker: A Biblical Guide to Resolving Personal Conflict, 3rd ed.* (Baker, 2004) as an excellent guide to reconciling with your spouse and others. While you and your spouse should digest the whole book, it's vital at this point for you to read chapters 1-6, especially chapter 6 on the "7 A's" of confession.

7 This could include your children (their age and their knowledge of the event is critical), the spouse of the adulterous partner (considering 1 Thess. 4:6; Ex. 20:17), your church family, or your extended family members. Let your pastor or biblical counselor guide you.

8 I address the problem of wallowing in guilt over your past sins in my booklet, *Bad Memories: Getting Past Your Past* (CCEF Resources for Changing Lives Ministry Booklet Series, P & R Publishing, 2004).

9 For a comprehensive Bible study on forgiveness, consider Genesis 50:17-20; Psalm 25:7; 32; 51; 103:8-12; 130:3-4; Proverbs 19:11; Isaiah 1:18; 38:17; 43:25; 44:22; Jeremiah 31:31-34; 50:20; Micah 7:18-20; Matthew 6:12-15; 18:15-17; 18:21-35; Mark 11:25; Luke 17:3-4; 23:34; 24:46-47; Acts 2:36-41; 7:60; Ephesians 4:31-32; Colossians 1:13-14; 2:13-14; 3:13-14; and 1 Peter 4:8.

10 While using various terms, this twofold distinction is seen in Ken Sande, *The Peacemaker: A Biblical Guide to Resolving Personal Conflict*; Paul David Tripp, *War of Words*; Jay E. Adams, *From Forgiven to Forgiving*; and other biblical counselors.

11 Biblical counselors agree with each other that attitudinal and transacted forgiveness are required when the offender truly repents, and that marital restoration is the ideal outcome of the repentance-forgiveness process. They sometimes differ, however, on whether relational forgiveness *requires* the wife to recommit to the marriage or if she might in exceptional cases *choose* – wisely, prayerfully, and with godly counsel from others about the hearts of both parties – the divorce provisions in Matthew

5:32 and 19:9. The exceptional cases of course require much pastoral wisdom and careful assessment and counseling .

12 Ken Sande, *The Peacemaker*. Sande's volume is the best resource to help you forgive an offender and reconcile the relationship God's way. Other writers slice the same pie into three promises: I will not dwell on your sin; I will not use it against you; and I will not tell others about it. See, for example, Jay E. Adams, *From Forgiven to Forgiving*.

Robert D. Jones is Assistant Professor of Biblical Counseling at Southeastern Baptist Theological Seminary in Wake Forest, NC and previously served as Pastor of Grace Fellowship Church in Hurricane, WV.

Other Booklets

A.D.D.: Wandering Minds and Wired Bodies,
    by Edward T. Welch, P&R Publishing

After Adultery, by Robert D. Jones, New Growth Press

Anger: Escaping the Maze, by David Powlison,
    P&R Publishing

Angry at God?: Bring Him Your Doubts and Questions,
    by Robert D. Jones, P&R Publishing

Asperger Syndrome, by Michael R. Emlet, New Growth Press

Bad Memories: Getting Past Your Past, by Robert D. Jones,
    P&R Publishing

Conflict, by Timothy S. Lane, New Growth Press

Depression: The Way Up When You Are Down,
    by Edward T. Welch, P&R Publishing

Domestic Abuse: How to Help, by David Powlison,
    Paul David Tripp, and Edward T. Welch, P&R Publishing

Forgiveness: "I Just Can't Forgive Myself!"
    by Robert D. Jones, P&R Publishing

Forgiving Others: Joining Wisdom and Love,
    by Timothy S. Lane, New Growth Press

God as Father: When Your Own Father Failed,
    by David Powlison, New Growth Press

God's Love: Better than Unconditional, by David Powlison,
    P&R Publishing

Grief: Finding Hope Again, by Paul David Tripp,
    New Growth Press

Guidance: Have I Missed God's Best? by James C. Petty,
    P&R Publishing

Homosexuality: Speaking the Truth in Love, by Edward T.
    Welch, P&R Publishing

*"Just One More": When Desires Don't Take No for an
    Answer,* by Edward T. Welch, P&R Publishing

Loneliness, by Jayne V. Clark, New Growth Press